Lerner SPORTS

ALL-STAR SMACKDOWN

ANTHONY EDWARDS VS. DWYANE WADE

WHO WOULD WIN?

MATT DOEDEN

Lerner Publications ◆ Minneapolis

Lerner Publications Company
An imprint of Lerner Publishing Group, Inc.
241 First Avenue North
Minneapolis, MN 55401 USA

For reading levels and more information, look up this title at www.lernerbooks.com.

Main body text set in Aptifer Sans LT Pro.
Typeface provided by Linotype AG.

Editor: Anne E. Hill

Library of Congress Cataloging-in-Publication Data

Names: Doeden, Matt, author.
Title: Anthony Edwards vs. Dwyane Wade : who would win? / Matt Doeden.
Description: Minneapolis, MN : Lerner Publications, [2026] | Series: All-star smackdown (Lerner sports) | Includes bibliographical references and index. | Audience: Ages 7–11 | Audience: Grades 2–3 | Summary: "NBA guards Anthony Edwards and Dwyane Wade are both great scorers and leaders on the court. But which player is better in a head-to-head comparison? Explore their careers and stats and make your own decision"— Provided by publisher.
Identifiers: LCCN 2024038781 (print) | LCCN 2024038782 (ebook) | ISBN 9798765668498 (library binding) | ISBN 9798765683415 (paperback) | ISBN 9798765675892 (epub)
Subjects: LCSH: Guards (Basketball)—United States—Juvenile literature. | Edwards, Anthony, 2001-—Juvenile literature. | Wade, Dwyane, 1982-—Juvenile literature. | Basketball players—United States—Juvenile literature. | Basketball—United States—Juvenile literature.
Classification: LCC GV884.A1 D58 2026 (print) | LCC GV884.A1 (ebook) | DDC 796.3230922 [B]—dc23/eng/20240823

LC record available at https://lccn.loc.gov/2024038781
LC ebook record available at https://lccn.loc.gov/2024038782

Manufactured in the United States of America
1-1011543-53817-9/16/2024

TABLE OF CONTENTS

Dwyane Wade

INTRODUCTION

COMING UP CLUTCH

The Miami Heat were in trouble. The Heat trailed the Dallas Mavericks two games to zero in the 2006 National Basketball Association (NBA) Finals. Game 3 was critical. The Heat had to win.

Fast Facts

- Dwyane Wade was named Most Valuable Player (MVP) of the 2006 NBA Finals.
- Wade hit the game-winning shot in the first playoff game of his career.
- Anthony Edwards also played football as a kid.
- Edwards scored a career-high 51 points against the Washington Wizards on April 9, 2024.

Dallas led by 13 points with just six minutes to play. That's when Heat guard Dwyane Wade went to work. Wade drilled a shot from midrange. He made the basket, got fouled, and made the free throw.

Wade and the Heat kept attacking. With three minutes left in the game, Wade made a driving shot off the backboard. Then he scored on another jump shot. The Heat took the lead. Dallas had a chance to tie it with a late free throw. But the shot bounced out. Wade grabbed the rebound to give Miami a huge comeback win. The Heat went on to win the series. Wade was named Most Valuable Player (MVP) of the Finals.

Anthony Edwards

In 2024, it was Anthony Edwards's turn to be a hero. Edwards and the Minnesota Timberwolves (Wolves) faced the Denver Nuggets in the Western Conference semifinals. The Nuggets were the defending champions. They were expected to beat the Wolves.

But Edwards had other ideas. The 22-year-old guard was unstoppable. He drove to the hoop. He drilled long-range shots. On defense, he shut down Denver's star guards. With seven minutes to go, the Wolves led 82–81.

Edwards had the ball. He faked a drive to his left to get his defender off balance. Then he moved right and took the shot. *Swish!* Edwards did not stop. He scored 43 points and led the Wolves to a surprising win. They went on to beat the Nuggets. The win helped seal Edwards's place as one of the game's rising stars.

What would happen if Wade and Edwards played against each other? How would they match up? And which player would come out on top? Keep reading to learn more and make your own choice.

Edwards takes a three-point shot in a playoff game against the Denver Nuggets in May 2024.

CHAPTER 1

Dwyane Wade dribbles in a 2003 game.

OVERCOMING THE ODDS

Both Wade and Edwards had to overcome obstacles to reach NBA stardom. Dwyane Wade grew up in Chicago, Illinois. His mother struggled with drugs. When she ended up in prison, Dwyane went to live with his father.

Sports were an important part of Dwyane's life. He loved football and basketball. It was clear from an early age that he was a great athlete.

Wade went on to play college basketball at Marquette University in Milwaukee, Wisconsin. The head coach was Tom Crean. Wade became a star two-way player. He was great at both offense and defense.

Wade (left) takes direction from Marquette coach Tom Crean (right) on the sidelines at an NCAA playoff game.

CONSIDER THIS

Edwards wears the number 5 jersey to honor both his mother and his grandmother. Both of them died on the fifth day of the month. Edwards was also born on August 5.

In 2003, Wade scored 29 points in a shocking win over powerhouse Kentucky. The win sent Marquette to the Final Four. Later that year, the Heat chose Wade with the fifth pick in the NBA draft.

Wade in action on the court

Edwards on the court against high school rival team Heritage

Anthony Edwards also faced tough times during his childhood. He was raised by his mother and grandmother in Atlanta, Georgia. But both died of cancer when Anthony was just 14. His older brother and sister took care of him.

Sports were at the center of Anthony's life. As a kid playing football, he was a star running back. But he soon fell in love with basketball. He became the top-rated high school basketball player in the United States.

CONSIDER THIS

Tom Crean coached both Wade and Edwards in college. From 1999 to 2022, Crean coached at Marquette, Indiana, and Georgia. His career record is 403–306.

Edwards chose to attend the University of Georgia. Wade was one of his favorite players. Edwards wanted to play for Georgia coach Tom Crean in part because Crean had coached Wade at Marquette.

Edwards (left) listens to Georgia coach Tom Crean (right) in a 2020 game against Auburn.

Edwards goes up for a jump shot in a 2020 game against the Tennessee Volunteers.

Edwards played just one year at Georgia. He put up great numbers. But the team struggled. After the season, Edwards entered the 2020 NBA draft. The Wolves made him the first overall pick of the draft.

CHAPTER 2

Dwyane Wade celebrates after hitting a game-winning three pointer against the Golden State Warriors at American Airlines Arena on February 27, 2019.

TWO-WAY STARS

When he was growing up, Anthony Edwards loved watching Dwyane Wade play. It's no surprise that Edwards reminds a lot of NBA fans of Wade. Both are known for their high-energy style. They love to use their speed and skill to dribble past defenders. Their quickness and strength allow them to blow by defenders and get to the hoop.

In 2009, Wade showed off his offensive skill against the New York Knicks. He attacked the basket. He made jump shots. He even got hot from three-point range. Wade scored a career-high 55 points, and the Heat won the game.

Wade shoots against the Indiana Pacers at a Miami Heat home game.

In 2024, Edwards was just as good against the San Antonio Spurs. He was on fire from all over the court. Edwards made a scorching 59 percent of his shots. He had a career-best 51 points. The Wolves won 130–121.

Many star players focus on offense. But both Wade and Edwards are two-way players. They also put a lot of work in on defense. They are physical, high-energy defenders. This makes them even more fierce on the court.

Wade (left) defends against Milwaukee Bucks guard Monta Ellis (right) in a 2013 playoff game.

Edwards (right) drives to the basket in a game against the San Antonio Spurs.

Wade takes a jump shot in the Eastern Conference Quarterfinals of the 2013 NBA Playoffs.

Wade's defense was on display in a 2013 playoff game against the Milwaukee Bucks. Wade played like a star. He locked down his opponents with five steals and two blocks in the game.

CONSIDER THIS

Both Wade and Edwards have more than one nickname. Wade's nicknames include D-Wade, Flash, and Father Prime. Edwards often goes by Ant or Ant-Man.

Edwards showed off his defensive skills against the Denver Nuggets in the 2024 playoffs. Denver forward Michael Porter Jr. took a pass as he drove toward the hoop. It looked like an easy basket. But Edwards stepped in front of Porter. Edwards rose up for a thrilling block. It started a fast break that ended in a slam dunk for the Wolves.

Edwards (right) faces off against Denver Nuggets guard Kentavious Caldwell-Pope (left).

CHAPTER 3

Wade displays his gold medal from the 2008 Olympic Games in Beijing, China.

HIGH ACHIEVERS

Wade had a 16-year NBA career filled with both personal and team honors. He made 13 All-Star teams. He was the 2009 NBA scoring champion. He also won the All-Star Game MVP award in 2010. In 2023, he became a member of the Basketball Hall of Fame.

Wade still holds many records for the Heat. He played there for 14 of his 16 seasons. He won his first championship with the Heat in 2006. In 2010, he helped bring LeBron James and Chris Bosh to the team.

Together, the three superstars were called the Big Three. They won NBA titles in 2012 and 2013. Wade was also a member of the 2008 US Olympic team that won a gold medal.

Wade (left), Chris Bosh (center), and LeBron James (right) admire their 2012 championship rings.

CONSIDER THIS

Beginning in the 1980s, NBA players began coming together to form superteams. These teams have multiple big stars. Wade helped convince LeBron James and Chris Bosh to join the Heat and create a superteam.

Edwards is just getting started. He came into the league in 2020 at only 19. After a slow start, he showed his potential and finished second in Rookie of the Year voting. In 2023, he made his first All-Star team.

Edwards dunks the ball over the head of Toronto Raptors' Pascal Siakam during the 2023 NBA All-Star Game.

Edwards (center) plays in an exhibition game ahead of the 2024 Paris Olympics.

The 2024 season was his best to date. He was again an All-Star and became one of the league's biggest stars. After the season, he traveled to France as part of the US Olympic team. The team took home the gold medal, beating France in the finals.

Edwards lost his first two playoff series with the Wolves. But in 2024, he showed that he could lead one of the NBA's best teams. He helped score series wins over the Phoenix Suns and Nuggets. His great play gives Wolves fans hope for an NBA title in the future.

CHAPTER 4

Wade takes a shot for the Miami Heat in 2019.

AND THE WINNER IS

Who would win this battle? Edwards and Wade are alike in many ways. They have similar skills and approaches to the game. But there are differences between the two.

Wade was one of the best scorers in the game. If he got near the basket, he almost always made the shot. Wade was a smart playmaker. He was great at running the offense and making pinpoint passes.

In 2008–2009, he dished out 7.5 assists per game while leading the NBA in scoring with 30.2 points per game. His ability to score and pass made him hard to defend.

Edwards (left) and Wade (right) pose together at the 2023 NBA All-Star Game in Salt Lake City, Utah.

CONSIDER THIS

Wade played most of his career in Miami. But he also spent a season with the Chicago Bulls and one season with the Cleveland Cavaliers. Edwards has only played for Minnesota. He signed a contract to stay with the Wolves through the 2028–2029 season.

Edwards is a better outside shooter than Wade. Edwards often makes his three-point shots. He is also an electric dunker. He throws down power dunks that get fans cheering. In 2024, he thrilled NBA fans when he tossed the ball off the backboard and threw down an alley-oop to himself.

It's a clash between two basketball superstars. In a one-on-one game, the edge would go to Edwards. His strength and better shooting would be hard for Wade to handle.

But the NBA isn't a one-on-one game. Edwards is one of the league's rising stars. But he does not have the wins and numbers of his hero Wade. At least not yet. With three NBA championships and Hall of Fame status, Wade is the winner of this smackdown.

Which star guard would you put on top? Is it the young and exciting Anthony Edwards? Or is it the proven Hall of Famer Dwyane Wade? It is a tough call. Consider their strengths and make your own choice!

Wade shoots over the head of a Cleveland Cavaliers player during a 2014 game.

SMACKDOWN BREAKDOWN

DWYANE WADE

Date of birth: January 17, 1982
Height: 6 feet 4 (1.9 m)
NBA championships: 3
NBA MVP awards: 0
All-Star Games: 13

Stats are accurate through the 2023–2024 NBA regular season.

ANTHONY EDWARDS

Date of birth: August 5, 2001
Height: 6 feet 4 (1.9 m)
NBA championships: 0
NBA MVP awards: 0
All-Star Games: 2

GLOSSARY

alley-oop: a play in which a player catches a high pass and dunks the ball in one motion

assist: a pass from a teammate that results in a made shot

draft: when teams take turns choosing new players

Final Four: the last four teams in the college basketball championship tournament

free throw: an open shot taken from behind a set line after a foul by an opponent

guard: a player stationed in the backcourt, away from the basket, who directs team play

hoop: the rim of a basketball goal

jump shot: a shot in basketball made by jumping into the air and releasing the ball with one or both hands at the peak of the jump

playmaker: a player who creates open shots for teammates

rookie: a first-year player

LEARN MORE

Doeden, Matt. *Meet Anthony Edwards.* Minneapolis: Lerner Publications, 2025.

Flynn, Brendan. *The NBA Encyclopedia for Kids.* Minneapolis: Abdo Reference, 2022.

Jr. NBA
https://jr.nba.com

Minnesota Timberwolves
https://www.nba.com/team/1610612750/timberwolves

Sports Illustrated Kids: Basketball
https://www.sikids.com/basketball

Stewart, Audrey. *G.O.A.T. Basketball Shooting Guards.* Minneapolis: Lerner Publications, 2025.

INDEX

PHOTO ACKNOWLEDGMENTS

Robert Seale/Sporting News via Getty Images, p. 4; C. Morgan Engel/Getty Images, pp. 5, 7; John Biever/Sports Illustrated/Getty Images, pp. 8, 10; Al Tielemans/Sports Illustrated/Getty Images, p. 9; Kevin Liles/Sports Illustrated via Getty Images, p. 11; David E. Klutho/Sports Illustrated/Getty Images, p. 12; Austin McAfee/Icon Sportswire via Getty Images, p. 13; Michael Reaves/Getty Images, pp. 14, 29; Mike Ehrmann/Getty Images, pp. 15, 16, 18; David Berding/Getty Images, pp. 17, 19; Filippo Monteforte/AFP via Getty Images, p. 20; Ron Elkman/Sports Imagery/Getty Images, p. 21; Kyle Terada - Pool/Getty Image, p. 22; Ethan Miller/Getty Images, p. 23; Tom Szczerbowski/Getty Images, p. 24; Tim Nwachukwu/Getty Images, p. 25; David Santiago/El Nuevo Herald/Tribune News Service via Getty Images, p. 27; Victor Decolongon/Getty Images, p. 28.

Cover photos: AP Photo/Abbie Parr (Edwards); AP Photo/Tom DiPace (Wade).